HAUNTED CANNOCK CHASE

True ghost stories from the UK's spookiest location

By Lee Brickley

Contents:

INTRODUCTION

This book contains true ghost stories reported to paranormal investigator Lee Brickley by residents of the Cannock Chase district. Some names were changed to protect the identities of those involved, but everything you are about to read really happened according to those who told the stories. .

Cannock Chase is a twenty-six mile square forest in the heart of Staffordshire, England.

For generations, the area has been known as one of the spookiest and scariest locations in the entire country. It attracts ghost hunters and paranormal investigators from all around the world, and it's very hard to find a local who doesn't have a frightening tale to tell.

The Cannock Chase district encompasses the forest itself and a few surrounding towns and villages. Weird stuff happens everywhere there, and anyone who chooses to visit is just as likely to bump into a demon child with black eyes as they are to stumble upon a half-human pigman. You've probably read articles in the newspapers about those two, right?

Well don't worry, there are plenty of terrifying stories in this book that you will never have read before because this is the first time they've made it into print!

Some experts believe Cannock Chase is a paranormal portal area where strange and unusual entities can teleport into our world from theirs. It's an interesting theory, and while the jury is still out on that one, it would go some way towards explaining a few things!

The first paranormal events recorded in the area date back to the early 1800s, but many believe creepy things have been happening for much longer than that. Some even flirt with the idea that the portal at Cannock Chase was opened by a Celtic tribe called the Cornovii that lived in the woodland some two-thousand years ago.

While it's very difficult to prove anything one way or another, the stories in this book should leave you with no doubts about Cannock Chase's supernatural credentials.

Lee Brickley has been investigating shocking encounters in the Cannock Chase area for more than a decade, and his books on the subject have sold hundreds of thousands of copies all around the world. Lee continues to research and collect paranormal reports from Cannock residents to this day, and he uncovered a staggering 124 new cases of supernatural activity in 2022 alone.

Some folks claim Cannock Chase and the surrounding villages experience more unusual goings on than the fictional town of Hawkins in the hit Netflix TV show Stranger Things. By the time you get to the end of this book, there is a reasonable chance you will agree with them.

So turn the lights down low, try to ignore that thunder storm brewing outside, and allow yourself to reconsider everything you thought you knew about logic and physics.

Be prepared!

This is Haunted Cannock Chase.

Old Maggie at Pye Green

In 1964, Mildred Wilson and her husband Kenneth moved into a brand new house in the Pye Green area of Cannock Chase. The young couple were just married, and this was to be their first home, where they would eventually raise their children.

In those days, there were multiple housing estates in Pye Green, and the village was growing fast. The Wilsons' new property bordered the forest, and pretty soon after moving in, the loving couple began to take woodland walks on a daily basis.

It was on one such walk, a few months after their relocation, that Mildred and Kenneth had a very strange experience in the forest. It began with an eerie sound that stopped both of them in their tracks. Kenneth claims it sounded like an evil old woman cackling, but Mildred describes it as something far more unearthly. Regardless of the finer details, the sound was loud, and it frightened the couple half to death.

The noise lasted for around thirty seconds and seemed to be coming from behind the terrified walkers no matter which way they turned.

Fearing for their lives, Kenneth and Mildred ran home as fast as their legs could carry them. Neither of them spoke about the incident because they were so shaken, but over the next six months, the strangeness continued to such a point that it could remain unspoken no longer.

Mildred would always feel like someone was watching her when she walked in the forest, and Kenneth felt the same - he just didn't want to scare his wife by admitting it. Things got so bad the couple began to speak about the weird incidents with their neighbours. It was only then they met Cyril Gardener who owned a small, old house just around the corner from their own.

According to Cyril, the cackling that Mildred and Kenneth heard in the woods and the sense of being watched were definitely related. He told them a story his mother had told him about a malevolent spirit that haunts the woods in search of weak souls. The entity appears as an old woman to the victims she terrifies, and often creeps up on them before making her move.

Cyril's mother called her "Old Maggie."

She was allegedly cursed by a gypsy in the 1850s, and since then Old Maggie has been trapped between worlds, unable to pass to the other side until she collects fifty weak souls and breaks the spell.

In 1964, Cyril estimated that Old Maggie would have been around half way towards meeting her goal and lifting the curse, so surely she'd have moved on by now, right?

Wrong!

Shortly after the incidents, Mildred and Kenneth decided to

sell their home and purchase a different property in Heath Hayes where they both still live today. They never visited that part of Cannock Chase again, and so the couple managed to avoid any further upset. However, Old Maggie doesn't rest, and plenty of other people have encountered her since.

In 1986, two guys working for the Forestry Commission burst into their employer's offices with faces so pale they were almost transparent. The two men had been working in an area near to the Pye Green tower when they both sensed something was wrong. They heard muttering in the woods accompanied by a weird feeling that made goosebumps stick up on both their arms.

The guys tried to ignore the strange experience for a few minutes until they were left with no choice but to confront whatever was in the woods with them.

Shouting as loud as they could, the two men called out to the entity in an attempt to scare it away. Unfortunately, their voices had the opposite effect, and pretty soon they were being chased through the woods by something unexplainable.

"It was like a dark shadow that just kept moving closer and closer towards us. We ran like hell but it kept gaining ground until I tripped on a fallen tree and landed on the ground. Dave didn't notice I'd fallen, and so he continued to run all the way back to our van." One of the men wrote in a statement at the time.

"I managed to climb back to my feet, and I couldn't see the dark shadow anywhere for a few moments. Then I heard a twig snap on the ground behind me and the unmistakable sound of breathing. I spun around to see this ugly old woman standing right behind me. Her eyes were terrifying - like some kind of purple colour, and I froze for a second or two. That was when she opened her mouth and I saw it was full of maggots. I almost threw my lunch up. That's the last thing I remember before running back to the van." The Forestry worker continued.

Old Maggie is still very much around today, and so it seems unlikely she has collected enough weak souls to reverse her gypsy curse. Indeed, a group of teenagers loitering in the woods at Pye Green may well have encountered her as recently as 2022.

Mark, Sian, Kerry and McKenzie were hanging around in the very area where Old Maggie is often seen during their summer holidays from school. They often enjoyed chilling in the woods because there were no parents around and they could do whatever they liked. However, following their encounter, none of these teenagers dare go there again.

All four of them claim to have seen Old Maggie simultaneously when she appeared, just after dark, only a short distance from their homes in Pye Green. Luckily, they managed to get away and survive the experience unharmed, but something Old Maggie said sent shivers down their spine.

When the old woman's ghost manifested to the teenagers in the forest, she uttered the following blood-curdling words:

"Four weak souls…delicious!"

Needless to say, the teens had a lucky escape, and they've

been advised never to go to that part of the woods again.

THE PRINCE OF WALES PHANTOM

The Prince of Wales theatre in Cannock town centre is one of the most celebrated and frequented entertainment venues in the entire district. It has been that way for decades, and there aren't many people in the local area who haven't at least seen a Christmas pantomime there at some point in their lives.

What most folks don't realise, however, is that the Prince of Wales theatre is haunted by a frightening phantom that regularly traumatises both guests and staff. It's become somewhat of an open secret in recent times. Most people know about the paranormal happenings at the theatre, but there are only a few who dare talk about it for fear of making the situation worse.

Staff members are told to ignore anything unusual they might see during their shifts, and the general consensus seems to be that if they don't mess with the phantom, it shouldn't mess with them. Sadly, this logic is flawed, and supernatural encounters with this entity have been on the increase for some time.

On 23rd March 2011, James Gooch from Norton Canes claims to have seen the phantom in a window at the Prince of Wales theatre while walking past with his family. The guy says he had the distinct feeling someone was watching him before looking up and seeing a man dressed in black with a pale face staring back through a window on the stairwell. When James attempted to point out the shadowy figure to his girlfriend, it quickly disappeared from sight.

Three months later in June 2011, Tina Creswell from Hednesford claims to have seen something very similar. She visited the theatre to purchase some tickets from the box office and asked to use the toilet while she was there. The lady had the fright of her life when washing her hands as she noticed a man matching the same description standing behind her when looking in the mirror. She promptly spun around, but the dark figure was gone. Tina was so terrified by the incident that she asked for a refund on her tickets.

There are hundreds of people out there who all have similar stories, and new encounters continue to happen to this very day.

An ex-staff member, who for obvious reasons must remain anonymous, claims they would witness paranormal phenomena at the theatre on an almost weekly basis. Stacks of chairs would move across the building unaided, bottles from the bar would pop open when the room was empty, and the phantom would appear to scare the living daylights out of them.

The person in question says their experiences with the entity at the theatre came to a head one evening following a stage show performed by a famous psychic.

"The show went well, and some guests hung around after to meet the guy and take photos. The building probably emptied around 11pm, and I was supposed to clean up for the following day. I started to hear this weird, repetitive banging noise coming from inside the theatre which was odd because I knew it was empty," he said.

The guy then walked back inside the theatre and noticed a very heavy PA speaker bouncing up and down on the stage. As if by magic, the speaker would begin to levitate to a height of around three inches, and then come crashing back down to the stage around a second later. This was happening over and over again.

"I watched it for about a minute with my jaw wide open. I couldn't believe what I was seeing, and it sent shivers down my spine. Then it stopped. There was a couple of seconds of nothing before all the lights turned out and I found myself in total darkness. I panicked and started running for the door, but that's when I felt a presence very close to me. I can't tell you exactly how it felt. I just knew someone else was there," he said.

A single light then lit up the middle of the stage, and the theatre worker turned around to see the phantom standing right in the middle of the spotlight beam.

"I'd seen him a few times before this, but it was always in a mirror or a window, and he was only usually there a couple of seconds. This time he was right in front of me, and he was looking right at me. Suddenly I heard this evil-sounding pipe organ music that was so loud I instinctively covered my ears. It was like nothing I'd ever heard before so it's hard to describe, but it was piercing," he continued.

As the organ sounds began to fill the room, the pale-faced phantom threw his arms up into the air and started to rise up from the stage. The entire building shook as the spirit seemed to suck energy from the entire surrounding environment.

"The last thing I remember was running for the door and falling flat on my face as soon as I got through it. The manager saw me tumble and came to ask if I was okay. I was so shaken that I couldn't speak, but he could tell something was wrong, so he opened the door to the theatre to investigate. Everything was as it should have been. Nothing was moving around, the lights were all switched on, and the phantom was nowhere to be seen," the ex-employee said.

Needless to say, that guy soon made his excuses and found work elsewhere.

So who is the phantom of the Prince of Wales theatre and what does he want? Well, there are a few theories out there, but most people believe the spirit to be that of Harry Hosker, a degenerate wannabe actor who lived and died in the Cannock Chase area.

Locals who knew him say his acting skills were terrible, and he slowly became more and more bitter throughout his life following rejections from every single audition he ever attended. Many folks think his spirit attached itself to the theatre following a visit just before he died, and due to Harry's stubbornness and hunger for the limelight, they say it is unlikely ever to leave.

Whatever the truth might be, one thing is for certain, the phantom of the Prince of Wales theatre will continue to spook people for a long time to come.

GHOULS ON THE GOLF COURSE

Cannock Chase golf course is located at the rear of the town's largest park and is managed by the same folks who run the leisure centre and the Prince of Wales theatre. It's a popular spot for anyone with an interest in the sport, and the course is well-used on the weekends by many local people.

Originally designed as a small, 9-hole course, the site was expanded to 18-holes in 1992. Since that time, there have been lots of weird reports from golfers who claim to have witnessed paranormal activity, and some of them are downright terrifying.

What's most interesting is that many of these experiences seem to happen in precisely the same place on the course.

Those who use it regularly know to keep their eyes peeled on the 10th hole because that's where things tend to go down.

A gentleman from the village of Rawnsley who uses Cannock golf course at least a couple of times each month claims to have seen ghouls on the green on more than once occasion.

"I think it first started happening in the early 2000s. Some of the other blokes had joked about crazy things on the 10th hole, but I just thought they were having a laugh. The first time I noticed anything was while reaching down to remove my ball from the hole. As I leant forwards and began stretching down, I looked over towards my carry bag where my clubs were kept and noticed someone standing right by them. I couldn't tell you what they looked like as I only saw them out of the corner of my eye, but there was definitely someone there. When I stood up straight and turned around, they vanished," the gentleman said.

"Since then, I've had about ten encounters with someone or something I can't explain on the course, and it always seems to be in that same place. The scariest one only happened a few months ago. I placed my ball on the tee and took a swing but didn't manage to hit it. Then I looked down to see the ball wasn't there. I turned around and, just for a split second, I saw this guy was standing right behind me holding the ball in his hand. The shock of seeing him caused me to let out an involuntary yelp, and as I did, the man faded into nothing and the ball fell to the ground," he said.

The spooked golfer claims the ghost he encountered that day was about six-feet tall and wearing Victorian clothing. Although the spirit seemed to scare the man in question, he claims he could see a smile on its face, and that it didn't seem to mean him any harm.

"It's more playful than anything," the golfer said. "He just seems to like playing tricks on me and giving me a bit of a fright. I don't think he would actually cause me any harm."

While that ghoul of the golf course seems relatively benevolent, some other people who use the site have not been quite as lucky in their encounters. It would seem there is more than one spirit out there on the course, and some of them are a little more unfriendly than others.

In 2018, two Cannock men got a little more than they bargained for when attempting to sink their balls in the 10th hole. Roy Daily and Colin Davis were enjoying an afternoon playing golf in the sunshine when they were spooked by an entity determined to cause havoc.

"We were just about to take our last puts when loads of other balls started shooting out of our stand bags and landing all over the course. Neither of us knew what was going on. It was the strangest thing. We just tried our best to avoid getting hit on the head," one of them claims.

The pair of them then attempted to recover the balls from the course and return them to their golf bags, but it was no use. They would simply begin shooting out again a few moments later, and each time this happened, the force with which the balls shot across the course would increase.

"It got to the point where the balls were flying directly towards us as if someone was throwing them. I had bruises on my legs and stomach the following day, and my friend took a golf ball to the chin that knocked him clean out for at least a few seconds. We left the balls on the floor, grabbed our clubs, and got out of there. I saw something mad when I looked back towards the 10th hole though. This guy was just standing there pointing at us. He gave me the creeps," the frightened man said.

Members of the golf club tend to remain tight lipped about the paranormal activity there, but many of them have a story to tell behind closed doors.

Some people interviewed for this book believe that at least one of the spirits at Cannock golf course belongs to a man called George John Stubbs. He owned Old Fallow Farm which encompassed the ground on which the golf course sits today right up until 1870. It is thought he might be the Victorian gentleman people encounter so often. Allegedly, George was a very proud man who spent most of his life enjoying the land, so it makes sense that he wouldn't want to leave it after death.

When it comes to the other entities stalking the 10th-hole of the golf course, there is very little known about their potential identities. The only thing anyone can say for certain is that it's best to run away if they are ever encountered. The last thing anyone wants is to end up with injuries like Roy and Colin who were pelted, hard, by their own balls.

Cannock golf course is a great place to get some fresh air and burn off some excess energy, and nothing in this book should deter anyone from enjoying the site and making the best use of the local facilities.

Just be sure to avoid the 10th hole if you have a nervous disposition.

THE BLACK-EYED CHILD AT BIRCHES VALLEY

The black-eyed child of Cannock Chase is probably the most well-publicised supernatural entity that people are known to encounter in the Staffordshire forest. Some believe she represents the tormented soul of a little girl who was murdered in the area during the 1960s, but there are just as many other folks who suggest the black-eyed child is a demon or an alien.

She is often seen at Castle Ring, the iron age hill fort stationed at the highest point of the Cannock Chase woods. However, the following encounter occurred at Birches Valley during the summer of 2021 when two teenagers decided it would be a good idea to camp illegally in the middle of the forest. It was a decision they would soon live to regret.

Kylie Drakeford and Ben Tilly were both seventeen at the time of this incident, and they were very much in love. Due to the global pandemic, the couple were unable to see each other as often as they would have liked, and opportunities for them to spend an entire evening together were almost non-existent. That was until Ben came up with an idea. He grabbed his old tent from the garden shed and suggested they spend a night somewhere on Cannock Chase. Kylie thought it was the perfect solution to their issues, but things didn't exactly go according to plan.

Firstly, it was raining pretty hard that evening, and it turned out that the tent was less than watertight leaving the couple feeling rather wet and cold. Ben was smart enough to take some Gaffer tape, and did what he could to patch up the holes, but still the rain leaked in.

"It's still better than being without her," Ben remembers thinking to himself.

The couple zipped two single sleeping bags together for warmth and tried to stay as dry as possible. That was until around midnight when they both heard something moving around outside of their tent.

Believing it was probably deer passing through the woods (there are over 800 of them roaming free on Cannock Chase,) both campers remained as still and quiet as possible. The last thing they wanted to do was spook the animals as they might have become aggressive.

Ben realised something wasn't right when he listened closer to the noise. It wasn't a mob of deer at all. There was just one set of footsteps, and they seemed to be slowly encircling the tent. Kylie suggested they unzip the tent door to take a look, and Ben agreed. Slowly, he lifted the zip, and as the teeth separated and the door opened to reveal the dark Cannock Chase forest, both campers heard the unmistakable sound of a small child giggling.

Ben and Kylie immediately turned their torches on and began peering out into the shadowy woodland and calling out to what they believed must have been a lost child, but they couldn't see anything at first. Still, the giggling continued.

Ben was the first to notice something move from behind one of the trees surrounding their camp. Then Kylie caught a glimpse of the same thing. There was something out there alright, and it was running from tree to tree, hiding itself behind the trunks and occasionally peering out towards the couple. Neither of them could move their torches fast enough to keep up with it, and so they didn't get a decent view until it finally stepped out from behind a tree and stood in the clearing in front of them.

"I was absolutely terrified. I'd read the stories in the news about the black-eyed child, but it wasn't until the thing stood right in front of me that I could quite believe them. I knew instantly that we were dealing with the real thing because it moved in ways humans simply can't move. It was like it could teleport from one place to another when it was moving around and hiding behind the trees," Kylie remembers.

"I was shining my torch right at her and she just stood there staring at us with her head slightly dipped. That's when the giggling started to get louder and louder. It really sounded like it was coming from all around us even though I could see she was right in front of us. It was really disorientating for a few seconds. Then she bent down for a moment as if adjusting her shoes, stood back up, and ran off down a nearby path through a dense section of trees." Ben added.

The couple knew enough about the black-eyed child to refrain from following her back into the woods. Many people believe that she attempts to lead people away from the trodden path and into more isolated areas of the forest with the intention of getting them lost or causing them harm. Thankfully, on this occasion, the experience was almost over for Ben and Kylie. Had they chosen to follow the black-eyed child, things could have easily taken a nasty turn.

It was impossible for the young lovers to get back to sleep that night, and so they simply waited in their tent for the sun to rise, huddled together. It was only in the morning they noticed that things outside their tent weren't exactly as they left them.

At around 7am, Kylie and Ben bit the bullet and climbed out of their tent for the first time since the previous evening's supernatural encounter. They were both shocked to discover unusual piles of stones evenly spaced around the entire perimeter of their tent. There were also lots of strange stick formations hanging from the trees that looked a little like dreamcatchers.

The slightly shaken couple decided it was time to pack up and leave as soon as possible, and that's precisely what they did.

The walk back to Ben's car would take around fifteen minutes, and it was largely uneventful until he heard Kylie, who was only about three feet behind him, scream at the top of her lungs. Ben dropped everything and spun around just quickly enough to catch a glimpse of a small child with black eyes peering back at him from behind an oak tree. Ben shouted "leave us alone," grabbed Kylie by the hand and made the remaining short journey back to his car in double time.

A HAUNTING ON

SHOAL HILL

Cannock is a working-class town, and while there are also many middle-class residents these days, most families live in modest homes. There is, however, an area of Cannock reserved for those with slightly more cash in the bank, and that's the Shoal Hill.

It is not uncommon for houses located in this area to sell for millions of pounds, and so it should come as no surprise to learn that many of them even have snooker rooms and indoor swimming pools. To put it bluntly, it's where the rich people live.

The following encounter happened in one such luxurious Shoal Hill home during the winter months of 2016. The people involved no longer own the property, and so they felt confident speaking out about their experiences for the first time. For legal reasons, the exact address of the house has been redacted from this story, but it is one of the biggest and most expensive homes on the New Penkridge Road - so you can probably work it out for yourself.

The family involved consisted of a mother, father, and two young children. The events began, as these things often do, with something seemingly insignificant that might have gone completely unnoticed.

Molly and Michael are twins, and at the tender age of six they still shared a bedroom in the family home. It was the children who first alerted their parents to strange goings on when they informed their mother of a creepy knocking sound coming from inside the wardrobe at the bottom of their bunk beds. She investigated, of course, but could not determine the origin of the noise and presumed it must have been something to do with the water pipes in the wall.

The sound became much worse over the following few nights and prevented the children from getting to sleep. Their father Terry called a plumber to come and take a look but was told there weren't even any pipes in the wall behind the wardrobe, and so the pipework definitely was not to blame.

On the sixth evening of banging, young Michael awoke in the middle of the night to a terrifying sight. Sitting on top of the wardrobe at the bottom of his bed was what he believed to be some kind of monster. As the child was only six years old, he could do nothing other than scream and call out to his parents who soon came rushing into the room. The monster vanished.

Michael claimed that the creature sitting on top of the wardrobe had bright red eyes and was wearing some kind of dirty overcoat. His parents thought their son must have been having a nightmare, but when their daughter awoke screaming with a similar complaint the following evening, Terry and his wife Sarah knew something was very wrong.

Over the course of the next two weeks, odd things happened around the house. Family members would see a stranger in the bathroom mirror out of the corner of their eyes every time they walked past. When they would turn for a closer look, whoever it was would vanish. They would also notice a repulsive odour at random times during the night in different places around the home.

It soon became apparent to the entire family that they were experiencing supernatural phenomena, and so they called upon a local priest and asked for his assistance. While the godly man was a little hesitant to get involved at first, he eventually agreed to visit and bless the house.

Not a true believer in the paranormal, the priest was sceptical about the family's version of events, and he suspected there might have been a rational explanation for the strange goings on. Still, he went along to their home with some holy water and his bible in hand. In less than five minutes, the priest's whole perspective on the situation changed.

As is often the case with demonic activity, the frequency and intensity of the disturbances increased as soon as the man of god entered the house. By the time he spoke a few short passages from his bible, photo frames were flying off counters, cutlery was shooting across the room, and the children were becoming inconsolable. It was clear a demonic entity had attached itself to the Shoal Hill family, and it wasn't going to give them up without a fight.

Terry's wife and children went upstairs and locked themselves in the main bedroom while their father and the priest moved from room to room, cleansing the house and antagonising the demon. The holy man uttered verses from his book and sprinkled his blessed water all over the house. It seemed to be working. The paranormal activity seemed to be weakening. Then everything stopped.

Terry let out a sigh of relief, believing the demon had been vanquished, but the guy soon realised any celebration would have been premature. Just then, a very large and heavy book flew out of the bookcase in the lounge and smashed straight into the priest's head with considerable force, knocking him completely unconscious.

The man lay on the floor in the living room out cold as Terry looked on in horror. It was at that moment that the house appeared to suffer from a power cut. Everywhere went dark and it was impossible to see anything. A second later, as if by magic, the lights came back on and Terry noticed that the priest was nowhere to be seen. He quickly ran upstairs to check on his family and thankfully everyone was fine.

There were no more disturbances at the house in the six months following these incidents, but the family decided to sell and move somewhere new regardless. There were just too many freaky memories there and the kids would still have nightmares from time to time. They just needed a fresh start.

The weirdest thing about this story, perhaps, is that nobody can explain what happened to the unconscious priest who disappeared without a trace. Terry's wife called the number she used to contact him initially, but the line was totally dead; it didn't even ring. She then attempted to locate his name and parish online in the manner she had previously, but there were no listings. It was as if the holy man disappeared off the face of the earth, or even stranger, didn't exist in the first place.

It's possible he just got spooked and ran away during the

powercut, of course, but maybe, just maybe, the demon took his body and soul in exchange for leaving the family alone.

THE SMILING MAN

Near to the iron age hill fort of Castle Ring on Cannock Chase, there is a small residential area called Prospect Village. It's a tiny community with only a few houses and a village hall, and the people who live there have to walk a considerable distance along secluded roads if they wish to reach the nearest civilisation. It is on one of these roads that many people report having encountered a creepy entity that has become known as the Smiling Man.

In most of the accounts, people walking along the road out of Prospect Village see this "Smiling Man" walking towards them from the opposite direction. For those who know the area well, it might be useful to point out that folks tend to encounter him when travelling towards Rawnsley, with the smiling man moving in the opposite direction towards Prospect Village along the Cannock Wood Road.

The Smiling Man moves quickly along the path, and he is

very light on his feet, according to reports. Some witnesses claim they believe him to be some kind of dancer, with one claiming, "he moves a bit like Michael Jakson. Very fluid, rhythmic and fast."

As he approaches people and passes them on the street, the man gives witnesses a big, sinister smile, and they often report he has a crazed look in his eyes.

The scariest part of the experience comes a few seconds later when walkers turn their heads to take a second look at the strange man who just passed them by. Nearly all who encounter the Smiling Man report that his head appears to turn around 180-degrees. His body is still moving in the same direction, away from the witness, but his smiling face and crazed eyes are fixed on them. It is almost as if he can spin his head all the way around and face backwards.

While supernatural encounters of this nature might not seem to cause anyone harm, apart from freaking them out, there are some psychological aspects that could alter that perspective.

For instance, many of the people who bear witness to the Smiling Man in instances similar to the one described claim to suffer nightmares for many months after the encounter. A significant number of these bad dreams feature the Smiling Man himself, and he's usually chasing the victim in one way or another.

There are those in the community who believe the Smiling Man to be nothing more than a figment of the imagination. Many folks think that someone made the story up, and then everyone began talking about him and that somehow pushed the Smiling Man into the local psyche and brought it to life.

That's one theory, but the following story kind of blows it out of the water.

On 7th September 2021, Jemma Pew and her family moved to Prospect Village having purchased a new home there. None of them had ever visited the area before, and so they were entirely unaware about the Smiling Man and the paranormal encounters people have with him.

Three days later, on 10th September, Jemma left her husband and children with the intention of fetching the paperwork required to register at a local GP's surgery. Unfortunately, the battery was flat on her car and it wouldn't start.

Following a quick check of Google Maps, the lady realised that the doctor's surgery was only a short walk into Rawnsley along the Cannock Wood Road, so she grabbed her handbag and headed out the door.

The hard-working mother walked down the Cannock Wood Road towards Rawnsley and had a supernatural encounter with an entity that matches the description of the Smiling Man completely. She had never heard the story at the time.

Jemma first noticed the man in the distance, around two hundred metres from her position and moving towards her.

"It was almost like he was dancing towards me to be honest," she said. "He was kind of skipping and prancing around and I instantly felt a little scared."

As the Smiling Man and Jemma moved nearer and nearer to each other, the young woman's heart began to race, and that wide smile and crazed look came fully into focus.

"You're going to think I'm mad, right? But his face sort of looked similar to the big, smiling clown you sometimes see on posters when the circus comes to town. He just had this really intense look in his eyes as if he was about to explode," Jemma said.

As has become the norm in most Smiling Man sightings, the entity quickly passed the young lady without incident, and it was only when she turned around that something totally unexplainable happened.

Many other people who have encountered the Smiling Man claim his head somehow manages to revolve a full 180-degrees until it is facing in the opposite direction to his feet. The same thing happened in this instance, but then something different occurred. Unlike the others who simply saw the Smiling Man dance off up the road, Jemma claims he disappeared right in front of her eyes.

"It wasn't like he faded away or evaporated when I blinked or anything like that. He just stopped walking and some sort of black door appeared in front of him. He reached out, turned the handle, opened it and stepped inside. As the door shut, the whole thing vanished," Jemma remembers.

Traumatised by her experience and with a few chills crawling down her spine, the new Prospect Village resident decided to give the GP's surgery a miss for the day and head home. She told her husband about the experience but neither of them could come up with a rational explanation for what had happened.

It was a few weeks later when talking to a neighbour about the incident that Jemma first heard about the Smiling Man. The stories came as a bit of a relief to the woman because now she felt that the things she saw finally made sense.

Jemma's children are due to start at Kingsmead High School in September 2023, and the route to get there from home takes them along the Cannock Wood Road. Both Jemma and her partner have already decided they will pay for daily taxis when the time comes. Like so many others who live in the local area, they are now firm believers in the Smiling Man, and there's no way in the world he's ever getting anywhere near her kids.

FOOTSTEPS AT THE HOSPITAL

In 1870 an infirmary was built to help provide medical care to those in the employment of the Cannock Chase Workhouse. It was the first establishment of its kind in the history of the local area, and it paved the way for the founding and construction of Cannock Chase Hospital which first joined the NHS under the name "Chase Hospital" in 1948.

The building that stands on the hospital site today was unveiled in 1991, and since that time it has played a significant role in catering to the health needs of Cannock residents. There aren't many people living in the district who haven't used the services there on at least one occasion.

The hospital also provides a considerable amount of employment for the local community. Indeed, there is a whole team of cleaning staff tasked with keeping the place fresh and spotless every day, and it is some of those people who have the most interesting stories to tell.

There have been whispers about the hospital being haunted for many years, but nobody who worked there was willing to come forward and spill the beans. However, one former cleaning lady has bravely spoken out about the torment of her fellow staff members and the sheer terror they would feel during many of their late night shifts.

"I started working at the hospital in 1997 and stayed there until 2004, I think. My shifts were on a rotating pattern but I'd usually end up swapping with some of the other girls because it was easier for me to get there in the evenings," the lady said.

"I'd only been there a few weeks when something creepy happened. I was cleaning the floors upstairs and the place was empty, but whenever I turned my back towards the lifts, I would hear footsteps approaching me from behind. It really scared me to be honest, and I called out to see if there was anyone else around but got no reply," she added.

Events of this nature would happen on an almost weekly basis during her evening cleaning shift, and pretty soon the lady decided it would be sensible to speak to her team leader about it.

"I knew something was wrong the second I explained what had been happening during my shifts. She rolled her eyes as if it wasn't the first time someone had complained about things like that. She actually told me to just ignore it and get on with my work."

Over the next few months, the curious cleaning lady would hear the mysterious footsteps over and over again, and so she decided to conduct some experiments to see if she could work out what was really going on.

"I saw something in a film that gave me an idea. At the time, we were using a cleaning product that came as a powder. We would just mix it with water in a bucket and use it to scrub the floors. I decided to pour a load of this powder on the floor between myself and the lift. I then carried on with my work for a bit. When I finally turned around to take a look, there were clear footprints in the powder leading from the lift to around a foot behind me where the powder stopped," the lady remembers.

"It was incredible really. Then there was this one time when I was cleaning the lift itself with the doors shut and the lights went out as if there was a power cut. Something banged hard on the doors three times before the power came back on and I could finally escape into the corridor, but there was nobody there," she claims.

For a short period in 2002, the cleaning lady was asked to train a new recruit who claimed she was blessed with psychic abilities. The girl instantly said she felt the presence of a dark spirit on the second floor of the hospital, and she totally refused to do any work up there. Within a couple of weeks, she handed in her notice and claimed she "just didn't feel right" at the hospital.

There are also many reports of patients encountering supernatural phenomena at the hospital during opening hours, and almost all of the activity tends to focus around the lift and the second floor.

One lady claimed to step into the lift downstairs after a kind young man, who was already inside, held the door for her. He even pressed the button for the second floor. However, when the doors opened and the lady turned around to say thank you and goodbye, the man was nowhere to be seen.

A elderly gentleman visiting the hospital for a rheumatology appointment on the second floor said he got lost and asked a kind-looking male nurse for directions. The old man received the information he required, but as he watched the male nurse walk away, he claims the guy disappeared into the lift while the doors were still closed. He said it was like he could walk through walls.

So, are the footsteps that scare cleaning staff somehow connected to all the other paranormal encounters reported at Cannock Chase Hospital? It would be impossible to say for sure. Still, few people would be surprised to learn about such activity at that site.

While the current hospital does not provide emergency care or life-saving operations, there are going to be quite a few people who've died there over the years. It stands to reason that some of them decided to hang around. Maybe they got lost on their way to the afterlife? Perhaps they have some kind of unfinished business? Who knows?

The only fact anyone can know for sure is that people see strange things in that building that can't be explained rationally.

At the time of writing this, there have been no professional or amateur paranormal investigations at Cannock Chase Hospital, but that is something the author of this book would like to change in the near future.

The entire site is incredibly active, and with new spooky stories surfacing all the time, further research is most surely required.

CEMETERY SPOOKS

Opened in 1882, Cannock Cemetery is located on the Pye Green Road, and it is almost certainly the most attractive burial site in the entire district. While the cemetery is closed to new burials these days, there are still hundreds of graves there that local people visit every single week.

It should come as no surprise to those reading this book that Cannock Cemetery has played host to more than a few ghost stories over the years. Some folks claim to hear voices in the wind when laying flowers for their family members. Others believe there is a demon grave digger who stalks the cemetery during the nighttime. They say anyone who breaks into the graveyard and comes into contact with him will disappear forever.

It is even said that werewolves can be heard howling from inside the cemetery gates during a full moon, and that suspicious clumps of hair are often found on the benches and pathways.

While some of that might sound a little bit crazy, there can be no smoke without fire, and most experts are pretty certain there is a considerable amount of paranormal activity at the Cannock Cemetery site.

The following events happened one night at Halloween in 2021 and led to two teenagers willingly being blessed in a church for the first time in their entire lives.

Kyle and Charlie liked to spend their Friday night's drinking, and that usually meant sitting in Cannock park with their mates and a few cans. On this particular evening, however, the two of them decided it would be more fun to jump the wall at the cemetery and get pissed up in a spookier setting. It was Halloween after all!

Charlie and Kyle arrived at Cannock Cemetery at around 10pm and proceeded to climb over the wall and sneak inside. They weren't stupid boys, and they realised the importance of remaining out of sight, so the two of them walked to the middle of the graveyard where it was impossible to see them from the road. They found a bench and started drinking cans of Tennents Super.

Kyle told a ghost story his grandmother had told him about a spirit that lived in her house when she was little. Apparently, his nan could feel the presence for months before the entity finally revealed himself one morning when she was still in bed.

Kyle's grandmother, frustrated with the feelings of being watched, decided to call out to the spirit and demand it make itself known. A split second later, a tall old man appeared in her bedroom and began walking towards her bed. The entity then wrapped its hands around her neck and started to strangle her. If Kyle's great-grandmother hadn't heard the commotion from the next room, she might never have come to her daughter's rescue.

As a result of the incident, the family eventually decided to relocate to a different property. However, the people who moved into the haunted house after Kyle's grandmother and her parents were found dead less than six weeks later. The official cause of death for all of them was carbon-monoxide poisoning, but rumour has it that the entity killed them.

After hearing the story, the hairs began to stand up on the back of Charlie's neck. He felt uncomfortable and a little freaked out. Charlie got up from the graveyard bench and started to pace around. It was at that moment that both boys heard a weird noise coming from somewhere nearby. It sounded like moaning, as if someone was in pain.

"Hello?" They called out into the darkness, but there was no reply, just more moaning.

The lads decided to investigate, and so they placed their beers on the ground and began walking towards the sound.

Charlie and Kyle both saw something move from behind one of the gravestones, and then suddenly there was a voice in the darkness.

"You shouldn't be here. Disrespectful boys. Do you know what we do with scallywags like you?" The voice bellowed. "Come over here and I'll show you," it continued.

Without a second thought, the two young intruders started running. They ran as fast as their legs could carry them, and they were almost at the graveyard wall when a broad shouldered man wearing overalls and carrying a shovel stepped out in front of them.

"You can't escape me that easily," he said as the two boys stood there frozen and trembling.

Neither of them could see the man's face because it was too dark, but he seemed to be wearing some kind of overalls. The scary guy began walking towards Kyle and Charlie, all the time dragging his shovel on the ground which made a very uncomfortable sound.

"What do you want from us?" The boys cried out with the crazy shoveller only a few feet away.

"I want you and your kind to leave this graveyard and never come back," he replied while raising his shovel and pointing at the two young men.

They didn't need to be told twice, and so both Kyle and Charlie resumed their dash for the graveyard wall. The phantom gravedigger watched their every move carefully. Just before the boys reached safety Kyle noticed that Charlie seemed to vanish into thin air.

"Charlie? Where have you gone?" Kyle shouted in a panic.

"Down here," his slightly drunk friend replied.

Unbeknown to both of them, there were freshly-dug, empty graves near the cemetery wall, and Charlie had fallen straight into one of them. Kyle quickly bent down, extended an arm, and helped to lift his comrade out. Both of them then started to climb the wall as they heard the words "next time I'll fill it in with you boys inside," come out of the darkness.

While they had a lucky escape on this occasion, both Kyle and Charlie claim they will never break into the cemetery again after dark, and they strongly advise other people to follow their lead.

Did the boys really encounter a phantom gravedigger that night at Cannock Cemetery like so many others have before them? It would seem likely given their description and the dialogue spoken by the entity. However, spirits are often tricky and deceptive, and there are no guarantees they weren't dealing with something far more sinister.

Either way, anyone with sense will keep away from the graveyard at night because next time things could be a lot worse.

THE PIGMAN

STRIKES BACK

For those who are unaware of the Pigman that haunts Cannock Chase, it's sensible to begin with a short explanation of the creature and its origin.

According to local legend, the Pigman is a half-human, half-pig hybrid that stalks the woods and terrifies local residents after dark. Some believe it to be the product of a scientific experiment gone wrong, others say it's some sort of ghost or demon, but a few years ago, a gentleman who was stationed in the forest for training during World War Two came up with another, more logical story.

He said that military commanders were tasked with spreading misinformation in the local towns and villages with a view to discouraging people from wandering into the woods. They did this because there was a prisoner of war camp on Cannock Chase at the time, and the soldiers wanted to keep people safe.

The man alleged that he and a few others were told to spread the story of the Pigman monster in the hope of scaring folks away. Since that time, he believes the story has simply taken on a life of its own.

You can read more about the Pigman's origins in my books "UFOs, Werewolves & The Pigman: Exposing England's Strangest Location - Cannock Chase," and "Ghosts of Cannock Chase: Terrifying Reports of Paranormal Activity from the UK's Most Haunted Town."

The following incident occurred in the Summer of 2017 only a short walk from the Pye Green Tower.

Linda Mucklow and her partner Derek were walking their two dogs Barney and Fred through the woods just before sunset as they always did. It was a lovely evening, the sun was shining and the birds were singing. Both German Shepherds were having a whale of a time chasing each other through the dense trees.

It was around 8pm, and the sky was beginning to turn red. Derek and his wife were tired, and so they decided to turn around and start the journey back to their car. The second they changed direction though, Barney and Fred started to act a little weird. Far from being their usual excitable selves, the dogs seemed sheepish and timid, as if they knew something their owners didn't.

All of a sudden the couple and their dogs heard the distinct sound of a pig grunting and oinking away. They stopped dead in their tracks and glanced around to see if they could pinpoint the animal, but it was the barking from their dogs that told Derek and Linda which way to walk.

Closer and closer the couple moved towards the noise, but just as they seemed to be almost on top of it, the oinking stopped. It was as if the animal heard them coming and froze. They stood still for a moment and glanced around again. This time Derek saw something.

Around fifty metres from their position in the woods,

standing in between two rather large trees, was a figure they first believed to be a man wearing a pig mask. Linda called out to him and the figure started moving towards them. Forty-five metres, forty-metres, thirty-metres. As it moved closer It was becoming clear this was not a regular man in a pig mask. The couple began to recoil as their dogs Barney and Fred went crazy. Whatever this was, it wasn't good, and it looked very angry!

Derek and Linda started running with their dogs in the opposite direction with the swine-like monster trailing behind. Or at least, it was behind them for a while anyway. With less than two-hundred metres to go before the couple reached their car, the Pigman seemed to give up the chase. Derek looked back but he could no longer see the creature. Both he and Linda breathed a sigh of relief.

After a few seconds spent catching their breath, the dog walkers and their canine friends continued hiking back towards the car park. Their vehicle was in view when the Pigman stepped out from behind a tree and blocked their path. It was only around ten metres in front of them this time, and both Derek and Linda could tell they were dealing with something paranormal.

Barney was pulling hard on his lead and barking at the monster standing in front of them. In fact, he pulled so hard that his lead snapped and Derek could no longer restrain him. The German Shepherd lurched forwards and jumped up at the Pigman with a vicious attack. However, instead of connecting with the entity and causing some serious damage, the dog simply passed through him with no resistance at all before landing on his feet and looking rather confused. It would seem that, at least in this instance, the Pigman was not a flesh and blood being. For Barney to pass all the way through him in such a manner, he must have been more of an apparition than anything physical. Still, it's a pretty frightening encounter either way.

The Pigman let out a grunt and disappeared back off behind a tree. When Derek rushed over to check on Barney and see which direction the monster was headed, he was shocked to discover the creature appeared to have vanished.

The couple grabbed both of their dogs, climbed into their car and drove away. However, that was not the last time they saw the entity. According to Linda, she saw the Pigman one more time around three weeks later when walking the dogs on her own. She caught a glimpse of him in the distance but managed to get out of the woods before there was any interaction, which was probably a smart move.

There are so many sightings of the Cannock Chase Pigman that it's pretty certain he's really out there. Whether he's a half-human, half-pig hybrid, a shapeshifting demon or something completely different, most folks love to talk about their encounters and share theories.

We'll only know the truth about his origin when someone spends a little more time with the Pigman, but so far, nobody's been brave enough to hang around.

SIRENS ON HEDNESFORD HILLS

Hednesford Hills is a nature reserve connected to the Cannock Chase forest via some woods near Rawnsley. It is a popular location for walkers and ramblers, and during my teens at least, it was an excellent place to hide out when you were wagging school.

There is a racetrack at the top of Hednesford Hills where professional drivers come from all around the UK to compete. It has been open for more than fifty years, and the raceway offers the fastest quarter mile oval in the whole of Europe.

This story begins with fourteen year old Danny leaving Hednesford Raceway following an evening's entertainment in 2018. He attended the event with his friends from school, but decided to brave the short walk home alone as they all lived in the opposite direction.

Danny's parents owned a house close to Kingsmead High School, and so he should have been home in less than ten minutes. However, that short journey would end up taking Danny more than twelve hours due to a scary paranormal experience.

Once out of the gates of Hednesford Hills Raceway, Danny had to walk through the nature reserve to reach civilization. The distance was less than a mile, but the whole area was very dark and very spooky that evening. The young man walked briskly through the woods and towards his parents' house, but was soon distracted by an unusual sound coming from behind the trees. It sounded like a girl singing softly, and she seemed to have an exceptionally beautiful voice. Danny listened intently.

The boy switched on his phone's torch and began walking into a dense grouping of trees following the sound, but no matter how far he moved, the singing never seemed to get any closer. He scanned the woods in the hope of finding the girl and telling her that she had an amazing voice, when all of a sudden, the singing stopped.

It was dead silent for a few seconds, and Danny heard a soft female voice again. It said, "follow me." The singing then continued, and the young man did his best to keep it in ear shot, venturing further and further into the wilderness.

After five or six minutes, it finally seemed as though Danny was getting closer to the mysterious girl. The singing became much louder with every step he braved, and it sounded as alluring and bewitching as ever. In truth, the boy felt as though he had been placed under some kind of a spell. He forgot all about going home and developed a single track mind for locating the heavenly singer.

All of a sudden, Danny saw her for the first time. Dressed entirely in white with a daisy chain in her hair, the blonde maiden looked directly into his eyes and gave the confused boy a cheeky smile. "Follow me," she said again in her velvet tones.

Without a second thought, Danny edged forwards a couple

of steps but the floor seemed to disappear. The boy tumbled and began to fall head first off what felt like a cliff side. His body bashed into rocks as he fell around thirty feet before crumpling up as he hit the ground. Danny lay there unconscious for a whole two hours before finally waking from his daze and using the luckily undamaged phone in his pocket to call an ambulance.

So what happened to Danny on that night, I hear you ask? Well, it would seem he encountered some kind of siren. Not the type you might find on the top of a police car, but a siren like those mentioned in Greek mythology.

Usually in female form, these creatures were said to appear out at sea. They would entice sailors towards dangerous rocks that could sink their ship, and the entities would use their beauty to mesmerise the men before essentially killing them.

When the ambulance crew found Danny, he was at a place on Hednesford Hills called Kingies Rock. It is a large rock platform that sticks up out of the ground around twenty metres, and that's where the Siren must have been standing when it led the young man towards his fall. He approached Kingies Rock from the nature reserve which meant he was at the same height as the platform. Unfortunately, there was a massive sheer drop between him and it. As it was so dark, Danny just couldn't see that the ground had fallen away, and he was totally disoriented from the spellbinding singing.

The staff at the hospital were fantastic, and they soon patched the young man up and sent him home. Luckily, apart from a few nasty sprains and some cuts and bruises, Danny came out of the experience relatively unharmed. It's rather impressive really, as the boy fell from a height similar to that of a two storey house.

What's even more incredible is that Danny has heard the singing on three more occasions while walking on Hednesford Hills since that night, but has chosen to ignore it as much as he possibly could.

"I always make sure I have my headphones with me whenever I walk over there now. It really felt like the singing put me under the influence of something weird, so I just put my headphones in and turn my own music up really loud every time I hear it. It seems to work," he said during an interview.

"There was one other thing though," he continued. "When I got to the hospital that night, the nurses asked me to remove my clothes and wear a gown, right? I reached into the pocket of my jeans and pulled out a daisy chain just like the one the girl wore on her head. I have absolutely no idea how it got into my pocket, but there it was."

Perhaps the siren took pity on the young man and offered her headdress as a means of apology? However, that would seem an unlikely explanation given the way in which these paranormal creatures operate.

Danny has been advised that it's far more likely the beautiful maiden put the daisy chain in his pocket to remind him of her, and perhaps even mark him for future attempts on his life. Whatever the truth is, anyone walking alone on Hednesford Hills at night should keep their eyes and ears peeled.

In Greek Mythology, a siren only dies on the rare occasion when a mortal hears their song and lives to tell the tale. Danny is still alive, for sure, but the Hednesford siren is still out there somewhere too. That might prove she is far stronger and scarier than anything the Greeks encountered all those years ago.

SOLDIERS AT SHUGBOROUGH

The Shugborough Estate makes up vast swathes of land on Cannock Chase. The grounds are massive, and within them is a large stately home, most of which was constructed in the 1690s by a gentleman called Willian Anson.

Today, it is a popular tourist location as the manor house itself belongs to the National Trust, and so it is possible for anyone to visit most of the time. There are also many events held within the grounds every year that include pop concerts, a Halloween spooktacular, and more. If anyone reading this has never been there before, it's definitely advisable for a great family day out. The gardens are amazing!

Unlike many other paranormal reports from Shugborough,

the following account did not occur within the walls of the mansion. Instead, the story you're about to read happened within the extensive grounds of the estate, far away from staff members and excited visitors.

It actually happened during one of the Halloween Spooktacular events when elderly couple Frank and Joan Parker had taken a wrong turn and lost their way in the vast grounds. There was a ghost train attraction installed that year, and the couple were attempting to find it when they seemed to lose all sense of direction.

Frank was certain he could lead his wife back to the safety of the crowds, but no matter which way they turned, the pensioners just became more and more disoriented and lost. What made matters worse was that neither of them could use their mobile phones competently, and Joan hadn't packed her glasses.

"Let's just stop moving for a moment and think," Frank said to his wife. "I'm sure we can retrace our steps. That ghost train has to be around here somewhere," he added.

The problem was that Frank could not retrace his steps. It was very dark and the couple had wandered through some woods and had absolutely no idea where they were. Joan was beginning to panic but her husband attempted to calm her down with reassurance.

"If we keep walking in a straight line, we're sure to come across a road or path soon," he said.

Without warning, and as if out of nowhere, three men wearing bright red clothing rode past the couple on horseback. Frank called out to them but they didn't seem to hear before disappearing off into the distance. Joan highlighted the strangeness of the situation, and her husband just stood there puzzled.

"Why on earth would they be riding through the woods in the middle of the night?" He questioned.

Just then, another four men wearing the same bright red clothing came into view as their horses' galloping pounded the ground creating a noticeable vibration.

"Oi you lot!" Frank shouted at the top of his lungs. "We're lost and we need help."

This time the men appeared to hear him. They pulled on the reins of their horses and changed direction so the men were now riding towards Frank and Joan. They stopped only a few feet away and asked if they could offer any assistance.

"Oh yes you can, please," Frank said. "We lost our way and we can't get back to the Shugborough Estate."

It was then both Frank and Joan noticed the unusual clothing worn by the men on horseback. Not only were they in bright red uniform, but they wore big leather boots and carried swords at their sides.

One of the men spoke.

"Take a left at that big ash tree over there, and you'll be back at Shugborough in no time," he said. "Now we are really very busy sir. There is a war on, don't you know, and the King has sent for us. We leave for France in the morning."

The four men then bid Frank and Joan farewell before riding off into the distance with haste.

Sure enough, the elderly couple did find their way back to the Shugborough Estate by following the directions given to them by the mysterious men on horseback. They decided to locate their car and drive home straight away after their fright in the woods, and thought it best to leave the ghost train that year.

It was only when the couple arrived home that Frank began to research the history of Shugborough. He found a lot of information online, but nothing helped him to make sense of the words spoken by the men in the woods. Then the old man came across a photograph that made his blood run cold. Not only did he find an image of men wearing the exact same uniform as those he met, but he was convinced the guy who spoke to him was in the shot.

The problem? It was an artist's impression of a battle from the Nine Years War (1688-1697) which was ongoing in Europe at the same time as the Shugborough manor's construction. Frank did a little more research and discovered that landowners from all over England were asked to send men to fight in the war which many consider to be the first ever global conflict. He showed the image to his wife who also agreed the man they met looked strikingly similar.

Could it be possible that the horse riders Frank and Joan encountered that night at Shugborough were the spirits of soldiers sent by the previous owner of the estate to fight and die for England in the Nine Years War? Potentially. It is also possible they were spirits from any year between 1645 and 1897 because that is the time period in which the British Army wore their signature red coats.

While Frank and Joan's experiences in the woods weren't particularly dangerous for them, and the spirits they encountered appeared rather friendly, the couple say they will stick to daytime events at the Shugborough Estate in the future. That's probably for the best considering their poor sense of direction and inability to use a mobile phone to call for help.

"If only I'd have realised they were ghosts at the time," Frank said in an interview. "I'd have asked them to tell me next week's lottery numbers."

His wife rolled her eyes. "They're ghosts, Frank. They're dead. They don't know anything about the future. You're getting confused with fortune tellers again," she replied.

The Rugeley Radio Messages

Rugeley is a small town on the edge of Cannock Chase where few exciting things ever happen. It's a nice-looking place with two train stations, lots of pubs, and some very large housing estates. It used to be home to the iconic cooling towers of Rugeley Power Station which dominated the Cannock Chase skyline for more than fifty years until their demolition in June 2021 (there's some cool videos of that on YouTube if you're interested.)

While life in Rugeley is often slow, there are sometimes incidents that liven the place up a little. The Rugeley Radio Messages had such an effect.

Over the course of a single week in 2022, Brady Morris and around thirteen other people living in the Rugeley area received a series of eerie, sinister messages through their FM radios. Something appeared to be interfering with the signal and disrupting regular programming for short periods, but it only seemed to be happening within the same two-mile radius. Plenty of people outside of this area did not experience the same phenomena.

There were those who thought the broadcasts were some kind of hoax, and those who believed them to be from another time, but only one thing was for certain, the radio messages were seriously spooky!

Brady awoke on 3rd March 2022 at his home on the Peartree estate in Rugeley. As was his usual routine, the guy climbed out of bed and into his slippers before heading towards the bathroom to wash and brush. It was a morning like any other, but within ten minutes, Brady would have a rather unusual experience that would leave him feeling oddly perplexed.

Brady walked downstairs and into his kitchen to prepare breakfast. He turned on the radio, as he always did, and heard the familiar sound of a famous BBC Radio 2 presenter's voice. They were reading the news headlines as the guy made himself a cup of coffee and waited for his toaster to pop.

All of a sudden, the radio seemed to lose signal, and there was nothing but white noise to be heard. Then, out of the static came a quiet voice that relayed the following message:

"The portal is now open. The invasion has begun."

Brady couldn't believe what he was hearing but within a few more seconds BBC Radio 2 was back on the air. He instantly wrote down the message so as not to forget it, and continued getting ready for work. For the life of him, the guy couldn't work out what the message might have meant.

After work, Brady went to sink a couple of pints at the Ash Tree pub which was only a few minutes walk from his house. While in the bar, he happened to mention the odd radio message to the landlord who informed him someone else relayed the same story earlier in the day. So Brady knew for certain that other people experienced the same phenomena. He left his number with the landlord and asked him to pass it on to his friend who also heard the message.

Brady arrived home around midnight feeling rather drunk. He crashed out on the sofa and remained there until the sun came up. The following morning, the guy began his usual routine and turned the radio on as soon as he made it into the kitchen. Just as Brady finished his last bite of toast, the BBC broadcast cut out again and another message came through.

"The portal is stable," the voice said before listing a series of numbers and letters. Brady wrote them down as quickly as he could. "52.7559° N, 1.9433° W." He then headed off for a long day at work.

Back in the Ash Tree pub that evening, the landlord contacted his friend John who agreed to come down for an hour to talk to Brady. He heard the strange radio broadcasts too, and both guys hoped they could get to the bottom of them.

It was John who first realised that the numbers and letters

Brady wrote on his notepad were map coordinates. He hadn't been fast enough to jot them down himself, but soon typed the code into Google to discover the location. Both men were shocked to discover that the coordinates pinpointed a spot very near to their current location within the grounds of Rugeley Leisure Centre.

"That's really weird," John said, feeling confused. "Why would the messages talk about a portal at Rugeley Leisure centre? It makes no sense," he added.

Word soon spread in the local area about the radio messages, and other people began to come forward claiming they heard the same things. There were now a small group of them at the pub every night discussing the day's messages and their theories about them.

There was a new broadcast coming through the radio every morning for the next five days, and most of them seemed to refer to what the voice called an open portal at the map coordinates of the leisure centre.

The group of curious local people decided it would be

sensible to visit the exact map coordinates and check things out for themselves. They did that on 9th March 2022 at around 9pm at night. There were fifteen of them in total, give or take, and to any observers they might have looked somewhat like an angry mob. Still, the gang headed to the leisure centre and the alleged location of the portal. What they saw was staggering.

Every few minutes, a swirling vortex would appear in mid air before a shadow-like figure would step through. The vortex would then disappear and the figure would begin to walk away before vanishing in front of everyone's eyes. This process repeated over and over leaving the puzzled onlookers with their jaws on the floor.

One of the group decided to get a little closer to the vortex. They moved towards it as soon as the spiral appeared and began running as soon as the figure stepped through. Something weird happened though. When that member of the group reached the vortex, it snapped shut while letting out the loudest noise anyone in the group had ever heard. John and Brady honestly thought their ear drums had burst. Then nothing. No more vortexes, no more figures. After about an hour, everyone went home with more questions than answers.

Each member of the party listened carefully to their radios the following morning but there was nothing unusual. No strange messages, no map coordinates, just BBC Radio 2. They did the same thing every morning for the next few weeks but never heard anything ever again.

Many of them believe their radios somehow tuned into a supernatural frequency, and the figures they saw stepping out of the portal at Rugeley Leisure Centre were spirits or demons. I suppose we'll never know for sure.

A Multi-Storey Mystery

The multi-storey car park in Cannock Town Centre is old and ugly according to most people, and that is why it is due to be demolished soon after this book is released. Indeed, most of the people who read this will never be able to visit the structure for themselves, but that's probably a very good thing if the following story is to be believed.

Children who grew up in the 90s and 00s would spend a lot of time "dossing" at the car park with their friends because it provided some shelter from the elements, and they were mostly left alone. The following incident occurred in 1999, but there are plenty of other similar reports from much later, some as recent as 2021, and they all follow a similar narrative.

This incident involved three teenagers called Mat, Sandy and Rich who got a little more than they bargained for when hanging around smoking in the car park's extensive stairwell. It was the best place to hide out, or so they thought, because the stairs were used infrequently by the public thanks to the installation of a more convenient elevator.

The young trio were laughing, joking, and smoking lots of cigarettes in that stairwell for hours before anything strange happened. In fact, it wasn't until they attempted to leave the area that Mat, Sandy and Rich encountered supernatural phenomena.

The boys had decided to exit the stairwell on the first floor, and so they climbed down the old concrete stairs and pulled at the door handle. Surprisingly, what greeted them on the other side was not the first floor at all. It was actually the second floor as the numbers on the wall inside the car park stated.

Presuming they made a mistake, all three boys re-entered the stairwell and walked down another flight of stairs. This time, opening the door left the teens totally speechless. As impossible as it sounds, and as unsettling as those lads found it, the fact was; they were back on the second floor of the multi-storey car park.

"What the hell is going on?" Mat said, looking at the other two boys. "We were on the second floor last time, and we just walked down more stairs. How are we still on floor number two?" He continued.

Sandy and Rich couldn't find the words to reply. They just stood there shaking their heads and wondering if they were on some kind of a trip.

This time, the teenagers walked all the way to the bottom of the stairs. That should have meant they passed the first floor and were now on the ground floor which leads out to Cannock Shopping Centre. Again, they opened the door, and again, the same unexplainable event occured. It seemed that no matter where the boys attempted to leave the cold stairwell, they would always walk out into the car park on the second floor.

"Let's just get out here and walk down through the car park," Mat said. His friends agreed, partly because they felt as though they didn't have any other choice.

The multi-storey itself was completely empty that day, or at least that was the case on the second floor. The three lads made their way towards one of the ramps that vehicles would use to drive between floors, and then something even stranger happened.

A single car appeared out of nowhere and began slowly moving towards them. It was a big, black Mercedes with huge rims and blacked-out windows. The boys jumped out of its way but the car stopped alongside them and a window came down.

"Do you need a ride?" A voice said from within the vehicle. Sandy peered inside but was unable to locate the driver. The car seemed to be empty.

"Do you need a ride?" The voice said again as if out of nowhere.

"No thanks we're good," Rich replied to the seemingly invisible man.

The window on the Mercedes then rolled up as the boys heard the final words, "suit yourselves."

The car started to move forwards and all three boys watched as it headed for the next ramp along which would have taken the driver to the third floor of the car park. Except, that's not what happened.

Whoever was behind the wheel didn't make the turn, and it seemed as though the big, black car was about to smash into the wall of the multi-storey. The boys held their breath in anticipation of the loud bang that was sure to follow, but it never came.

While it may sound crazy, and plenty of their friends make fun of them for telling the story; the teenage trio claim that the car passed directly through the wall with no resistance at all. There wasn't a brick out of place or a shard of glass on the floor. It was as though either the car or the wall had been a hologram.

Sandy rushed over to the brickwork and began slapping it with his hands. "Did you two just see that?" He said, feeling totally spooked. His friends just nodded their heads.

"We've really got to get out of here," Rich added before grabbing both of his friends and heading for the elevator. "We haven't tried the lifts yet," he said, "let's see if they work."

Thankfully, the lifts did work, and the boys managed to get themselves to safety. Mat pressed the button for the ground floor, and when the doors finally opened, there was an old couple waiting to get inside.

"You boys look like you've seen a ghost!" The old man exclaimed after setting eyes on the three lads. Mat, Sandy and Rich looked at each other before turning back to the couple.

"I think you might be right this time," Sandy replied, followed by a long breath of relief.

The old man and his wife began to laugh before entering the elevator as the teens walked out onto the street.

"Stay safe you four!" he shouted as the lift doors closed.

The three lads felt a little confused by what the old man said. At least, that was the case until they walked past a shop window and saw an unidentified extra person in the glass accompanying their reflections.

Spirit of the Subway

The subway that leads from Morrisons car park into Cannock Town Centre has always been a hive of activity. It's a busy route accommodating those who mischievously park their vehicles at the supermarket to avoid paying charges in the town, but there are some excellent buskers who perform down there occasionally too.

The walls of the subway are tiled, and Cannock Council makes an effort to ensure they showcase the town and the talented people in it. For instance, at the time of writing this, there are many original works of art printed onto the tiles, and the subway serves as a kind of free art gallery.

While it's only a small tunnel that a person could walk through in less than a minute, sometimes the journey can become rather terrifying, especially during the early hours of the morning as many local people report.

There seems to be some kind of paranormal activity happening down there involving the spirit of a young man who allegedly enjoys tormenting walkers and scaring them out of their skins.

On Saturday 24th November 2018, Molly and Vicky were walking home from a bar in Cannock Town Centre to Heath Hayes. It is a rather long walk of at least a couple of miles, but the pair of them were drunk, and they didn't have enough money left to pay for a taxi and get a kebab. Unsurprisingly, they chose the kebab.

The girls walked through the grounds of St Luke's church and passed the little community centre built at the side of the 12th century religious structure. They followed a short path and were soon near the entrance to the subway. As they were both a little worse for wear, the decision was made to take the ramp down, rather than the steps.

Molly and Vicky were giggling and messing around right up

until the moment they began to walk through the tunnel and instantly heard loud footsteps right behind them. The girls turned around but there was nobody there.

They looked at each other with puzzled faces, but that just made them both start giggling again. Perhaps if they hadn't been quite so drunk, the girls might have been a little more prepared for what would happen next.

As they continued to walk through the tunnel, the footsteps started again, but this time neither Molly nor Vicky would turn around. They just quickened their pace in the hope of reaching the exit before anyone could catch up with them. Then, all of a sudden, a young man appeared in front of the girls, blocking the path.

"Have you two had a good night?" The sharply-dressed man said in a friendly voice.

Molly replied that they had a fantastic night, and all they wanted to do now was get home.

"Why don't you just stay here with me?" The man

questioned before lifting his arms from his side and allegedly levitating at least a foot from the pavement. "I could show you some tricks," he continued with a devilish smile that now dominated his face.

For want of a better term, the girls crapped themselves, dropped their kebab, and began to run back towards the other entrance to the tunnel. As they did, the young man appeared in front of them yet again and said, "I told you I could show you some tricks," before bursting out into an almost psychotic-sounding fit of laughter.

"Just leave us alone, okay?" Vicky shouted while Molly began to visibly shake.

Yet again, the girls changed direction and attempted to leave the tunnel via the exit that would take them onto Morrisons car park, but also yet again, the frightening man who appeared to have superpowers blocked their path.

Molly was having none of it. She grabbed her friend's hand and charged at the young stranger. "Move out of our way or I'll mess you up," she shouted while quickening her pace and running straight for him. The guy looked a little surprised at their reaction, but not as surprised as Molly and Vicky were when he suddenly vanished before their eyes just before the point of impact.

Both girls made it home safely that night, and there were no more mishaps along the way. However, no less than six months later, a woman called Sandra Howell endured an almost identical experience in the subway, but it doesn't stop there.

Throughout 2020 and 2021, there were no less than eighteen reported sightings and encounters with the spirit of the subway, and witnesses range from school children to pensioners. Many of these folks don't know each other, and until this point, the story hasn't been widely publicised so it is very unlikely they made these sightings up.

So far, the entity stalking that tunnel hasn't managed to cause physical harm to anyone, but all indications suggest that it is only a matter of time before something far more terrible happens. What if someone stays and agrees to see some more of his "tricks?"

Hopefully nobody is ever stupid enough to find out.

A Ghostly Encounter at Slitting Mill

Slitting Mill is a small village on the edge of Cannock Chase near to the town of Rugeley. It's a quiet place with some very nice houses and lots of countryside to explore. Apart from only having around two hundred residents, Slitting Mill is home to an excellent pub with fishing pools to the rear called The Horns. There's also a waterfall in the area, although that can be difficult to find and those planning to visit are advised to use Google Maps.

There is a lot of ghostly activity in Slitting Mill for such a small place, but the following story stands out from all the others. It involves an old lady called Beryl who has lived in the area since she was a little girl. Her encounter began one Sunday morning while washing up the dishes and gazing out of her kitchen window.

The window overlooked Beryl's beautiful garden where she would spend many hours during the summertime, but as it was winter, the old lady was lost in thought, planning which flowers she would plant the following year. It was then she noticed something move out of the corner of her eye. Whoever it was appeared to have walked past her kitchen door and into the living room. Beryl jumped a mile and the washing up water went everywhere, but she quickly dried her hands, grabbed a rolling pin, and went to investigate.

The shaken woman presumed someone had broken into her home because she was the only person with a key. She began to call out as she slowly edged through the living room door to greet whoever was inside. To her amazement though, there was nobody there.

It's worth explaining that Beryl was seventy-two years old at the time of this incident, and she was prone to making mistakes and getting confused. Seeing there was nobody in her home, the old woman thought her mind must have been playing tricks, and so calmed down a little and went back to her washing up. Two minutes later, the same thing happened again.

"I must be going mad," Beryl thought as she picked up the rolling pin for a second time and ventured into the living room. This time though, she saw something, and the horrifying sight caused the old lady to let out a shriek.

He was only there for a moment, less than a blink of an eye, but Beryl saw a very nasty-looking man standing behind her when she glanced into the living room mirror. He wore a black top hat and his face looked weathered and rough, but it was the man's eyes that really sent a shiver down Beryl's spine. They were entirely bloodshot apart from a small yellow patch in his left eye that appeared to be seeping some kind of puss.

The old lady was now petrified. She wasn't a firm believer in the paranormal, but she knew what she saw, and there was no other way to explain her encounter. Thinking quickly, Beryl picked up her telephone and called her friend

Suzan who the woman knew would sometimes visit psychics. She hoped Suzan could offer some advice or at least put her in touch with someone else who could.

Maybe it was just one of those weird synchronicity things, but Suzan answered the phone by saying "Beryl, how are you dear? I was literally just dialling your number."

The two women spoke about the incident and Suzan promised to send her medium friend Karen over as soon as she was available. Beryl thanked her and waited patiently for the next three hours. She didn't move from her armchair in the living room for the entire time as she was too scared of what might happen.

When Karen arrived at the house, she could sense there was a presence in the home immediately. After some kind of spiritual meditation, she even managed to describe the appearance of the entity to Beryl without being told what he looked like.

"That's incredible," said Beryl, "how on earth can you know what I saw?"

Karen went on to explain that she didn't want to alarm the old woman, but the ghost has never left her living room. He'd been there with her the whole time.

"I saw him as soon as I walked in," Karen said, "I just wanted to be sure."

Just then, a loud banging started on the fireplace wall that made the mirror actively shake. It continued for around thirty seconds until the frame came away from the nail and the mirror smashed into a thousand pieces on the floor. Karen explained that she needed to work quickly because the spirit was becoming angry.

"This is not a normal ghost," the medium explained. "It's far more powerful than that and it wants to hurt you for some reason."

Karen then held both of Beryl's hands and began chanting the Hanuman Chalisa, which is an old 16th Century Hindu devotional hymn said to help protect against evil spirits. As the medium made her way through the whole forty verses of the passage, everything in the house started to move around. First the chairs and sofa flipped over, then the expensive vases on Beryl's coffee table smashed against the wall. It was complete chaos.

Just as Karen reached the last verse of the Hanuman Chalisa, a photo frame containing an image of Beryl's late husband shot across the room and hit the medium on the head, knocking her unconscious. At the very same moment, the scary-looking man appeared in full form right in front of the old lady. He looked into her soul with those bloodshot eyes and Beryl suddenly began to choke. She had severe difficulty breathing and it felt as though someone had their hands around her throat, squeezing very hard.

The scary man's gaze became even more intense as Beryl began to lose consciousness. Things could have been a lot worse if Karen hadn't woken up at that moment and finished the fortieth verse of her mantra. As the last syllables left her mouth, the old lady felt the grip easing around her throat, and soon she could breathe again.

The man in the top hat started to fade away, but not before

speaking out loud for the first time. Just before he vanished from the old woman's living room, the entity said, "I'll get you back one day for what your husband did to me." Then everything was calm.

A couple of months after the paranormal encounter, and with the events of that day still fresh in her mind, Beryl decided she would attempt to work out what the spirit must have meant with his final words. She spent weeks sorting through all her husband's old paperwork before coming across a photograph of a man who looked strikingly similar to the entity that invaded her home. He was standing next to her husband in the picture, and the words "Great Wyrley, 1973," were written on the back.

Suddenly, it hit her. She knew exactly who the scary man was, and it made her blood run cold.

While her deceased husband was a kind man to most people, he had another side during his younger years, and would often try to avoid speaking about a particular incident that happened before he married Beryl and moved to Slitting Mill.

His best friend Charlie died in a weird accident in 1974 for which the explanation never seemed to make any sense. Beryl's husband was never charged for any crime, but he was considered a suspect by many people.

Given the experience the old woman had with his spirit in her house that day, she is now 100% convinced her husband had a few more skeletons in his closet than she realised.

THANK YOU FOR BUYING THIS BOOK. NOW CHECK OUT SOME OF THE OTHERS AVAILABLE FROM AMAZON.....

If you would like to contact Lee Brickley for any reason at all, please do so by emailing:

leebrickleyauthor@gmail.com

Printed in Great Britain
by Amazon

21025762R00071